GOLDEN MEMORIES OF LIFE

FRIENDS- FUN -CLASS - MEMORIES

T.KRISHNA DINESH

Copyright © T.krishna Dinesh
All Rights Reserved.

This book has been published with all efforts taken to make the material error-free after the consent of the author. However, the author and the publisher do not assume and hereby disclaim any liability to any party for any loss, damage, or disruption caused by errors or omissions, whether such errors or omissions result from negligence, accident, or any other cause.

While every effort has been made to avoid any mistake or omission, this publication is being sold on the condition and understanding that neither the author nor the publishers or printers would be liable in any manner to any person by reason of any mistake or omission in this publication or for any action taken or omitted to be taken or advice rendered or accepted on the basis of this work. For any defect in printing or binding the publishers will be liable only to replace the defective copy by another copy of this work then available.

I would like to thank everyone.

Who are sincerely book lovers?

My family and friends.

Finally to my caring, supporting and loving parents my deepest gratitude. Your encouragement when the time is tough is much appreciated and duly noticed.

MY Heartful thanks.

Contents

Foreword

To The book lovers,

I hope this book helps you to get you out of your work and take you to the world of love.

I would love nothing more than seeing the book in your hands everywhere —Readers walking down the streets, the browser's in a book store, at home.

That's a great challenge which lies ahead of me but it is certainly worth an attempt.

Take out time from your busy schedule to rejoice.

Hope you read and Enjoy.

Preface

This is tale of the college life phase which has abundant memories and which cherish the beauty of the college life. Most of the moments occurred in this tale are from the experience of my own and rest of the characters are my classmate and friends of mine.

Although my book is intended purely for bring back the memories of the college life phase of everyone who has cherished many beautiful moments in their life.

Acknowledgements

"I would like to take this opportunity to thank my publishing team."

"Thanks to everyone on the Book in the team who helped me so much".

I cannot express enough thanks to my book team for their continued support.

I offer my sincere appreciation for the learning and opportunity

Prologue

This is a work of my own experience in college life.

All the characters depicted any resemblance to real person or dead is purely coincidental.

The content of the book reflects the author expression and opinion solely.

This work doesn't not claim scriptural or identical authenticity.

CHAPTER ONE

ENTER OF COLLEGE LIFE

12 June 2018 :

This is the day when I first started my college life. I have travel around 1 hour reach the college from Dilsukhnagar to Mehidipatnam to reach my college it was repudiated Business school. I first have to catch a auto for 2 km then I have reach a signal cross the road then catch running bus then I have stand for nearly half distance to get a seat.

Then I met a guy name Bala Prasad in the RTC bus he greeted me and asked where I am going for 2 minutes I was silent cause I won't speak to strangers then I spoke to him. Then we headed to the college way then I told name we just give a smile gesture.

We headed to college entry it was great feel to enter college premises it was great feel and small fear inside how will I do this it's a business school and I barely know English. Based on the graduation they have allocated the sections like engineer student one class and degree students one class.

Then I asked the classroom way then I went into classroom which has almost 60 students. Section is "C"

.There is place in last bench beside a guy who is bold and with great well build body his name is Ravi at first I just greeted him sat beside him listened to class.

For a couple of class after we got brake time then I went to canteen to know what they sell and meet the owner of the Canteen called Ashwin & Dattu brother I had some coffee and egg puff for the first day there.

After brake I and Ravi started talking and ignoring the class and chitchat. Like that lunch time came I went outside for food met Bala again we both spoke about class and I had fried rice many of our college students came there I made some classmates there.

On that evening I went to ground to go in college bus I enquiry in the office room which route to Dilsukhnagar and what is the bus number they said bus number was 1. I boarded the bus and sat in bus observed the route and stops which place will wait.

I boarded in my stop which is sagar ring road and have to get a share auto if it's not available I have to walk 2 kms I walked and reached my house the day has happened well.

13 June 2018 :

The next I went to bus stop saw some girls stand at a point I dint understand where will bus stop I was very tense then after a while then a girl near the stop with goggles has spoken to me are also student of the and waiting for the bus I said yes then & then I saw our bus and boarded the bus then I got to know the girls who boarded the bus also were my classmate and my batch mates .

After a while I saw the faces of all bus mates and started to get connected slowly then among the bus mates I have becomes friends with "Madhu", she is the girl who is come late to the bus stop I will ask the driver to wait for her and guy name "Harsha" who is crazy and have good sense of humour and who is obsessed with tik tok at that time.

Then at Karmanghat bus stop I met guy name "Shiva" who has positive Aura along with time we become good buddies with no time we use to bunk class too. When shiva & I bunk class we never get caught but when my others friends bunk the class they get caught next day they use to get punishment to write something related to the their class should show it to their class.

But we had luck so we use escape and go and sit class. Many of our friends feel jealous of me and shiva for escape of punishment after some class. Shiva was my bench mate so I and Ravi and shiva used to sit side by side shiva use to listen class while Ravi and me use to chit chat and look at watch.

On that evening after college class we use to meet at ground and wait for other sections to meanwhile we use to look at girls. Observe them then I start communication with our bus mates slowly over the time.

I Made friends with "Malathi,"Darshana" & "Mahmuda","Pravalika".

Among them "Malathi" is very close to me we use eat at same table we use be very close she one kind of unique whom we can rely anything. Then there is "Darshana" who has some positive aura and multitalented she is best company one can have in their life. "Mahmuda" we call her hybrid girl she was one of the best person I ever mate who is kind of silent killer initially we use have lunch together after section division time has changed. "Pravalika" she is chatter box but talks lot about books and studies but nice and good being sometimes she doesn't know how to tackle situations.

Kiran Mishra , Abhilash, Adrusta Deepak, Srikanth, Guru these are my buddies for the life we use to meet in the college canteen a lot by going late to class and they close the door then we meet in canteen and stay there for some time.

14 June 2018:

This day I met a girl today in bus top when bus was about to leave I saw a girl came running but this time she was not Madhu & someone new girl whom I don't know. She is boarded later we start our journey to college. Later I got know her name as "Hasini". we can say she is pop star kind of girl cool simple & clever and sometimes stubborn too but very emotional being.

Later at Iso stop I saw tall and bold girl who has great smile and positive vibes who is may be 5'8 height her name Is "Teju" who is cool girl. "Teju" is paka Telangana girl over time she became a good friend to me we use to talk a lot sometimes we use to listen too in bus sit beside also she is best person whom we can rely for lifetime.

On that we college they said the rules on this like clean shave and formals for boys with shoes and tuck later they said of the rules of college then how many subjects and all on hearing for 2 years they will be 54 subjects I got shocked and start to think can I finish them is that easy oh my god! Can I complete them how do I make this work all this running in my head. For year 3 trimesters they said on hearing this I said to myself I'm out.

This day everything was normal I got bored of class as they are saying basic introductions so I used to make friends in class with some guy from north "Summit" who is kind and simple Person within the time we became good friends.

He then introduced me to the "Kiran" who is like minded guy who is good buddy of mine we use to meet mostly in canteen with Tea and samosa and coffee slowly my friends list begin to expand.

15 June 2018:

On this day I use call my friends wait in bus top we use talk become buddies "Madhu" & "Hasini" became good friends in bus shiva and I use to became buddies we use listen songs together and after reaching college we use to chit chat for 30 minutes before college starts.

Sometimes we order at some place 70mm Dosa and eat in Canteen I and Madhu use to share it and we eat that Dosa and have some juice in Dattu brother Canteen.

When we get bore of class we use to go late if we go late the class teacher will close class door so we stay in canteen and enjoy some class and have fun joke. Sometimes when in charge come to check in canteen we use to run to toilets.

On this day I became friend with "Sreya" who is best friend of me smile face with fabulous eyes I like spending time with her. She is awesome buddy and best friend of mine I always felt happy around her.

Later in the evening it was raining full then we waited for some students but "Teju" "Madhu" & "Hasini" "Harsha" and along with me we all played in rain we took a lot of selfies too on that day.

Like that a week has passed I made many friends in my college days.

1 July 2018:

On this day it was Sunday I met few of good buddies and celebrated the birthday of the Sanjay & Darshana we met at a PVR near our college. On this day I met "Yash sharma", "Devanshu" "Sanjay" & Darshana." The birthday celebration of the "Sanjay & Darshana" we had chit chat and we had lunch and everyone has played some games in the games world and we had celebrate the birthday by cake cutting at the evening and we presented some gifts on that day to them we took few selfies also.

4 July 2018:

This is time when college has initiated the EDP program in the college. Entrepreneur development program was started. we are assembled in seminar hall 1 then Noor Farsistan class was started and we had motivation class and stories and divided into teams and had played some games for full day those are best days in the college life.

Initially I was team mate of Srinivas, Harshini, Prakash,Deepak, and Darshana, Mahumuda. We have named our team as "Magical Strings" We provide in can you feel is the caption for our team we have played well as team mate for that two days.

At the lunch time we all use to sit in Canteen and have food we use to share food and "Darshana" use to sing songs for us she got talent and when she use to sing I used sing also but my friends will ask me will please stop singing like that then I used to be silent.

Evening time we use to have fun in the ground during the bus waiting time we use to talk and meet and think what is this college and studies how we goanna make it to the final will we become post graduates like that.

9 July 2018 :

From this day on the real Entrepreneur development program was we were divided into teams and I met new classmates and friends at this moment "Syed Soyali","Abhishek chowdary" "Pooja" "Kunal" & "Aparna" we were made a team and we aimed to give our best and be perfect among the 250 members in the college.

I was poor when it comes to presentation at that time but I don't want my team to lose because of me so I did my best in the team to be honest the team was best even anyone join in my place.

In this competition we don't want to lose so we came up with new concept called fitness fusion energy drink which is made of fruits. And we named it as "Foozy The Fitness Fusion" tap into the beauty of infused water. India's first infused water premier company.

I gave my contribution in the team. Worked my best I use to mingle learn slowly English and how to be team player and what team goals are everything. I can say that during this time everyone in the college have been doing their contribution as team players and leaders and key supporters every must deserve an award but as we know it's competition so only some be winners.

When I used to get free time I use to sit beside my friends help them too. On this day I felt I met special someone. Our team use to plan everything be as team as if colour dress code and all.

CHAPTER TWO

Winner of Entrepreneur Development

11 July 2018 :

On this day we had to prepare the break-even point of the product in the market how we to deal with financial and all I the customer relationship manager while "Sohali" ,"Ankitha","Aparna", "Abhishek " ,"Pooja" "Kunal "everyone has prepared the ppt and all ready for the presentation.

Our presentation went well my team gave me boost and help to present like this and I did my part. We had prepared our sample I and "Aparna" are preparing the infused water for it we went to "Datta" bhai canteen while cutting the fruits we had little conservation I like the time we had and we finally prepared the infused water gave it to the Staff in our college.

They had give the feedback and complements also every other team was stunned by our performance and they said that your team will the winners of the competition for sure.

12 July 2018:

On this day we have prepared for the Edp program I had clean shave today with a tie formal white shirt as we all guys had plan to wear white shirt and boarded the bus at bus stop this day everyone in the bus was happy with smile faces I had taken couple of picture with "Hasini", "Teju" and "Madhu".

We had a fresh start I seen many lot of happy faces today I went to my friends team spend some time today before the program starts. I helped "Sreya" wished her all the best.

I prepared the cups and poured the infused water while "Sohali" cut the fruits into different models and shapes while "Aparna" and "Pooja" has prepared the water and many of the seniors came and saw our "Foozy" taste it and gave the marks.

That evening when everyone was assembled in the Seminar hall we have waited and hearing appreciated everyone and when our name came everyone has over joyed announced as all the credit goes the my team I did very little part and many who supported us this is first time i won in my life.

I was overjoyed and dancing inside after receiving the trophy I went to "Sreya" I took a selfie with her also taken the trophy from me every one of my team are so happy on seeing them happy it's the best moment for me.

We had great feast on that in "Datta" canteen on that before going home I saw all my teammates and thanked them and went with a happy face. I used chat with my teammates from that day onwards.

30 July 2018:

On this day we went to the industrial visit with Nagarajuna sir. Initially I sit with some of my classmates of girls we use to talk later in the bus everyone started to have fun play songs dance and enjoy.

Its my first time for industrial visit I used to see everything and excited like a kid. we went to Bisleri manufacturing unit I saw how bottle are made and how the bottle are filled and how the size of bottle are made and everything. I got clarified many doubts after visit of the plant.

5 August 2018 :

On this day we have to write exam at TCS office at hi-tech city at 12 clock we went to corporate office. It was first time seeing huge office like that other than in moves so I was watching and observing everything there. I have went mention floor to write Atma exam I wrote randomly exam without thinking much on that many of our friends been there.

After writing exam I start to observe the office and watching my friends they all are busy in writing the exams dead serious I was like is it that serious man really after that I open some cupboards and saw the files in the office read some but dint understand a thing so left them there.

After exam "Sreya" "Teju" "Viswa" is man of golden heart good buddy of us we use hangout less but he is best buddy one should have and "Ravi" in fiancé stream guy who lives in room was also with us and "Loya" who is singer of the college kind and man of simplicity we can. Later "Abhi" who is topper according to me who has some charisma and always smile at face attractive guy.

"Sreya" and I was on bike while "Teju" and "Loya" were on one bike rest of the our gang was on car "Ravi","Viswa","Abhi" were on car.

We went to restaurtent had some burger and sandwich and coke for all of us "sreya" took some pic with me and her selfies also later before we leave we all took group picture had a lots of fun.

We all went had some fun till evening and then we have went to our homes. That's how the day ended. It was great memories for us.

6th August 2018

From on this day I started chatting with "Aparna" I use to text her daily & I use to stare at her in canteen when I see her I get a strange feeling like some it make me happy. I can't express it in words I smile at her. I know that if I express this feeling to her she will not talk or be normal with me but fear let me stop expressing it. It's the most memorable day in my life. From that day onwards I started to love her and she has became an important person in my life.

10th August 2018

On this day I went to the 3BS for the first time in Hyderabad with my cousin whom I grew up his name is "Gowtham".He has introduced me to his friends "Yeshwanth" he is man with golden heart I use to call him "Yash dada".

I am elder than him so I use to share everything with him I use care also him so much even I use to share my sorrow with him I know that he will be a important person in my life. Sometimes I used to shout at him also but he never shout at me I use to get shocked how he manages he know a lot about the outside world than me I don't know anything much also because I don't have many friends and use to stay in home busy in my world.

He is sports person he plays cricket and football like pro player he also played for district also. So I went to 3BS we have order some non and veg and started enjoy the food their it was my first time at 3BS so I used to observe everything there drinks and food and environment after 3BS .

we went to charminar at 2 clock and had some chai and biscuits.

25th August 2018

On this day I felt I can't do this pgdm. I was unable to get anything into my brain I was upset angry and in frustration that day but it turned into beautiful day when I talk to "Aparna" in canteen had hope that I can do. And also I remember the insult which I had in my childhood that I won't qualify and pass degree so it had add flames and to never ever give up even if its tuff.

That I felt that I am crazy in love with "Aparna" but fear dint let me explain and express it. She is beautiful who is animals lover a lot like chocolates she even cares for her some she meets she traditional, spiritual, she is simply person one can make others happy and cherish the life.

CHAPTER THREE

Fresher's Party at Aalankrita Resort & Convention Hyderabad

7th September 2018

On this day I was all excited woke up early in the morning, got ready, reached the college hostel, and met my friends Yash sharma, Prajith , Summit, and surya. We waited for the college bus on the ground and boarded the bus has taken a lot of pics. Once we reached the resort we reached to the venue and had a welcome drink later we had a fashion show and some dances and songs by the seniors on the stage.

Later we went out and started to take some pictures with our batch mates and friends and well-wishers. When are friendly with everyone you have a lot of circles to talk and speak to and be with them. Koti Kiran, Abhilash, Satish, shiva, Kiran Mishra, Ravi, sai Kiran, Bala Prasad, and Sneha Tripathi in the fresher party. I was close to some girls too so I had taken picture's with them too.

Then I saw my girl in the green-yellow mix saree with the classic traditional look I was looking at her like that for a while then I went to her talked with her and ask for a selfie pic and took a pic. Later we had lunch the food was really awesome and then after that, I took some pictures with my friends.

In the evening we had DJ songs and we dance a lot and had the best days of our life.

18ᵗʰ October 2018

In this month I went for the trip to Tamilnadu from Hyderabad on the bus it was the long bus journey I ever had for a lifetime it was 2 days long journey I saw the places and all journey Evening I reached Trichy town from Hyderabad.

The place is very hot in the daytime and at night time it's very cold Trichy is famous for its educational institutions and university and is one of the holy places and I have visited many places in Trichy. I spend a week in Trichy in Tamilnadu and came back to Hyderabad.

9ᵗʰ November 2018

On this day I went night out with my cousin Gowtham, Yashwanth, Ranadeep, to Charminar and Tank band for the first time I saw Mata Maha Lakshmi temple in Charminar the devotees come a lot only at night time it will be for a week.

Then I had some Irani chai and some biscuits near Charminar then we took some selfies and went to the temple. Then we went to the Tank band and had some ice cream there spent some time there went to Ramki Bandi and had some masala dose.

12ᵗʰ November 2018

On this day I and my cousin had planned for Anthagiri hills lake for campfire it was an unexpected trip Gowtham and Yashwanth, Randeep, Rana, Varun we went in a car we started at 8 p.m. at night we bought some food and drinks and some we use Gps and reached there at around 11. p.m.

Started to collect some wood for a campfire and started to drink and had some food and we dance around it and saw the moon and talk many things it was one of the best memory. Later in the early morning, we reached home around 8 in the morning.

1ˢᵗ December 2018

On this day I volunteered and organized the "International Conference on Contemporary HRM Practice's" it was the first time in the ICBM-SBE College first time ever I had conducted organised the event. I felt great and happy on that day.

15ᵗʰ December 2018

On this day I told to Aparna that I like her so much in the call we talk on call barely for 5 times in the 2 years we only text a lot. She avoided me and blocked me for 3 months I was sad when it was happened.

29ᵗʰ December 2018

On this day I participated in the 6ᵗʰ International Case conference on "Managing Business in the Era of Disruption"

CHAPTER FOUR

A TRIP TO REMEMBERED PUNE & LONAVALA

April 30th 2019 :

NagaArjuna sir and Shubham were college official plant visit and manufacturing it was a great trip for a lifetime for us. The Acumen & connect was the organization which took us on the trip on the 30th of April 2019 we boarded the train in Hyderabad at 11:20 morning and I saw my angel coming on to trip I was all excited and when she came it felt great on seeing her after months and I was smiling.

we sit in the compartment, the whole compartment was full of our friends and classmates we started singing talking and started our vibes of the trip. I was with my buddy Adrusta Deepak, and Rajesh, Viswa, Pavan, shiva, and Nagaraju started talking.

The Naga Arjuna called some people and asked will you coordinate with the programs on the trip I kind of felt cool and I said I'm in and he gave us some instructions I copied them by mistake and send them to the group members then I got some scolding from the Naga Arjuna sir.

May 1st 2019:

We reached the around night at 2 clocks. They arranged the local buses we boarded the bus and we started to enjoy singing and dancing all on the bus and making fun.

They arranged OYO Flagships lions-den it was a villa so they gave 1 house for 20 members and that night they made the campfire everyone was celebrating at the campfire dancing many have been there as I was tired I left after some time and slept.

Early morning around 4 clocks we gather and then we started hiking I was in front and saw the beauty and nature many of them took selfies and made video boomerang. We reached the top and saw the sunrise and we felt great it was a great moment for us.

May 2nd 2019:

After the hiking, we came and had breakfast and we had idly dosa and sweet and some juice then we started our journey to Lonavla on the bus we were again full and went to the plant that day M.R.F manufacture Pune.

We saw how tires are manufactured and in the manufacturing sector, robots are used in manufacturing the tires. Milk plant production and different types and that afternoon we had pizza.

May 3rd 2019:

On this day we went to the small mall in Pune. I and Niharika, swati,Amulya,Pujith Nagaraju,Ashiwine,Ajay,Sushmitha. I met them first on this day she was one of my close buddies.

We went to a famous palace called Gandhi National Memorial Society & Aga Khan palace.

On this day I saw my angel in a white dress so happy to see her like that I felt great which words can't describe. On the bus, we all danced laughed and spend a great time.

We went to the Imagica water-park. We got into all ride and one incident we boarded the giant wheel on the building we can see the whole city from it and my friend was so scared he started to shout to stop the ride that's was the funny moment.

Till evening the whole day we spent there and that evening we played in ice park on Imagica park we all had great fun it was my first time playing in the snow later after playing in snow my body was literally shivering.

May 4th 2019:

On this day we went to Phoenix Mall which is the biggest and most famous mall in MH area some of my friends went to the pub and had some drinks and were literally dazed and dizzy on that time.

Then that evening we boarded the train everyone was tired and slept silently.

May 5th 2019:

We reached Hyderabad in early morning at 6:30 AM. We took and reached our homes.

A great trip with beautiful memories in the college life...

After the trip everyone was busy with to get into internship with the respective Specialization.

CHAPTER FIVE

SPECIALIZATION AND CAREER CHOOSING TIME

May 9th 2019 :

On this day we choose our respective specializations I was into Human Resource Management and many of my friends choose Marketing and some others into Financial Management.

As we choose our career path our class have been changed and you people always fear the new change as it was a human tendency I was so tense and have small fear inside me as I was a human being.

May 10th 2019:

In Human Resource Management, I and another guy were the only boys in class rest of the class were girls.

Their names are Sai Krupa, Mahalakshmi,varshini & Sakshi, Praveena, Swati, Niharika, Pranathi, Rashmitha, and Vyshanavi. Initially, I was shy later we all got along with each other best buddies forever. We all use to talk and sometimes we watch movies in class in the projector.

May 12th 2019:

I started my internship in a Reputation organisation. Before I got the internship I had an interview with the manager and he asked a few questions about what I know and tested my theoretical knowledge and gave me the offer of the internship.

During this time my Angel once again contacted me as she messages to me like hey! How are you? on seeing that message I was so happy. It was one of the best moments in my life.

May 17th 2019:

On this day we went to our director's granddaughter's marriage it was unexpected for me to go to that marriage there were numerous food items and I saw celebrities who attended the marriage function. I had tasted different types of food for the first time in my life.

That day I and my sir had taken about the struggle in life I learned there is a lot more to go in this life.

June 11th 2019:

I was happy on this day as I received my first salary in my life I was so happy on seeing the check it made me cry emotional and I went to the bank and deposited the check money I got.

August 29, 2019:

On this day our HR family has gone for a trip and event from our college to some HR convention meetings we always spend our time as they are our precious moments in this world.

We went to Telangana forest academy & Research academy which is far off from Hyderabad like 75 km which took us 1 hr and 45 minutes in our college bus and the area is Dulapally.

We started at morning 10 clock from the college reached there like 11;40 AM to the forest academy. We had walked about 2 kms in the academy saw many trees & plants and climbed a huge rock and took some pictures saw the view it was breath taking view.

CHAPTER SIX

FRESHER DAY PARTY FOR JUNIORS AT FORT GRAND

September 27th, 2019:

On this day we started at 10 AM for the fort grand with all my buddies and juniors on the college bus it was 1 hr journey from our college to fort grand which is 15 km located at Siddulagutta, Shamshabad, Hyderabad.

On entrance to the fort we had some drinks then we sat near my friends after 10-15 minutes I spoke to my friend Ravi to let's go out and take some selfies then it all started I took pictures with all most everyone in my batch and had some best memories in the wish list.

Satish, Prajith, Nadeem, and shiva has done a dance performance on the stage with some rock-level energy. Later in the evening around 4 clock, we started the DJ dance non-stop everyone in the auditorium started dancing and like anything even our sirs also started dance like non-stop for 1 hour we dance with full energy.

September 28, 2019:

It was Saturday when we had some fun watching movies on the projector and talking with one and all. We took selfies on the mobile some of my friends were busy with their laptops as they were it, professionals.

October 3, 2019:

It was teacher's day on that day . we called our HR Gurus and had planned a cake cutting our staff are very special they teach us the moral of the life and even great thing in life we are grateful for that in life.

We thanked them with our heart full wishes and made them cut the cake and gave some small part in the college. Later we had some fun at college.

October 10, 2019:

This time we are serious about our career & and busy with the mock interviews and preparing for the placements and our gurus used to help us to a great extent which we can't thank ever.

October 11, 2019:

This day we have gone through many mock interviews & we are confident that we can get placed everyone has done a marvellous role and is prepared to do well in the mock interviews.

October20,2019:

It was a Saturday week off I had drunk after many years we had some DJ and camp fire and talk about our emotions and all with my hostel buddies which made us become close.

It was a memorable moment in one's life.

November, 2019:

We had fun days as always in college life and spend the time with lots of memories as usual as normal days for us.

November 11, 2019:

On this day I went to Barbecue which is in Inorbit mall with my hostel buddies sai, Surya, shiva,Nadeem, Mahesh, Prajith, Satish, Devanshu, Guru, Akhil & Sravan we had the best food and spend quality time there and went to our rooms had some party.

CHAPTER SEVEN

KERALA TRIP WITH FRIENDS

November 18th 2019:

On this day my Friends Prajith, Satish and I went for a trip to Kerala we initially booked a sleeper coach but our lucky we got an A/C coach it was we started at morning 09:17 AM it was 10 hours journey.

November 19th 2019:

We reached early morning at 05:35 AM we took some lockers and got ready at Ernakulum town Railway station. We took some car travels for a week it was around 4k and self-drive first we started waterfall Athirapally Tourism information and centre at 09:05 AM.

Athirapally waterfall was the most beautiful sight-seeing ever we took some pictures like photo freaks.

At 11:20 AM we had lunch at Angamaly I burned my tongue at that cause Kerala people will drink hot water I dint know that so I drank fast and burned my tongue.

By the evening we saw Blossom Hydel Park& Munnar Flower Garden. After that we decided to see the Munnar highest peak "Idukki" - 1,532 m sea level we can see the clouds and we bought some chocolate and it was 39km from Munnar.

At 9:00 PM we took a hotel at Aluva for the night and we reached a room it was surprising to see there is no fan in the room later at late night the climate is so cold that we literally shivered in cold.

November 20th 2019:

In the morning around 07:46 AM we started at Aluva and started to Kundala Dam reached the dam at 09:43 AM later after a 1-hour drive we went to Munnar Tent Camp.

At the Munnar tent camp, we had some snacks and took some pictures with a tea garden in the background.

At 1:30 afternoon Paingottoor we had lunch and from there so we went to Kollam beach we played in Kollam beach and we saw another beach Venjarammoodu and at night we took night halt at Trivandrum.

November 21st 2019:

We went to the temple in the Trivandrum at the temple only traditional dress is allowed like men Dhoti and women with saree are allowed we have taken blessings from the lord and started to Alappuzha Beach.

Alappuzha Beach was a beautiful scene with coconut trees single road & beach astonishing view.

Our night stay was at Alappuzha Beach lighthouse we stayed that night in the car and slept like babies. That night police came for petrol and asked what we are doing he understood we are tourists and said don't go near the beach at night.

November 22nd 2019:

The next day at Alappuzha or called Alleppey we contacted some boat house and we went on the boat. We went on a black water tour on the boat it was a beautiful view and we enjoyed it a lot.

Love is the most best and dangerous thing ever in a person's life it can make him or break him one should know how to face it if its heartbreak.

Sometimes you don't know what to do after the heartbreak...so you just keep waiting and waiting that someone will come and rescue you from this loneliness but no one will come this is the harsh truth of life.. So, cry as much as you want and then wipe your tears and be strong and move on heart breaks are part of life.

The worst feeling isn't being lonely. It is being forgotten by someone you would never forget. The greatest weakness of human beings is their hesitancy how to tell others how much they love them while they're alive.

April 25, 2020:

On this day I finally had called my HR family after many months everyone and I missed them much but I never told them that till now I was not broken even my love is gone but I was scattered when people I love has been busy forget me can't blame them can understand.

September 17, 2020:

I went to my grandfather's place where my childhood was bliss with my cousin& his friends. I went to our paddy field and played there the place felt like heaven the smell of the air and soil everything was different there was actually heaven.

October 3rd, 2020:

This is the time when I use to go with my hero (my daddy) along with him to the duty places and know how the business and job go in an MNC company I learned a lot of things.

I got know how much pressure he faces in his work career and how tuff to balance career & family life.

November 7th 2020:

This is the first and foremost day when I started of thinking writing books and just gave a chance and took the step ahead then I learned how to write what are need?

How to start? Which is way how do I make? Many questions then I met a stranger in a app of mental health who has guide me and I am in debt of him he said and suggest how to start what to do and all.

Then I started writing books my first book was about the king of Lanka.

December15th , 2020:

On this day I went to Mantralayam ,Manchala famous temple of Lord Raghavendra swamy it is his Mutta, his life & work at the bank of river Tungabhdra River. The journey was really awesome while in the journey I saw deer & Peacock the bus route will be awesome with cool climate it is 13 hrs journeys.

It is one of the Vaishnava pilgrim's for the saint Guru Raghavendra swami

CHAPTER NINE

THE CONVOCATION CEREMONY EVENT

February 5th 2021:

I started my journey from Rajamahendravaram to Hyderabad for the convocation ceremony. Time has really flown so fast I was thinking of did I do it did I achieve it really like many thoughts are running in my mind, meanwhile I was on the journey.

February 7th 2021:

It was the day finally when we did it achieved graduation. Finally, we all did it HR family. Another day was added to the list. What I would do without them I felt that on that day love you so much.

After the convocation, I have given some gifts to my friends and we went someplace and had some food. That day I feel proud that I have achieved something great in my life and that I am not a loser anymore.

Tears started rolling in my eyes I couldn't stand on the ground I was in joy and crying then I saw my friend and went to them and we had taken some selfies. The day ended well.

College life experience is truly one of a kind. The most common memories people have of college life are definitely goofing around with friends.

They remember how the group of friends walked around the college in style and played silly pranks on each other.

Moreover, people always look back at the times spent in the college canteen. It was considered the hub of every student where they enjoyed eating and chatting away with their friends.

The annual fest created so much excitement and buzz amongst the students. Everyone welcomed other colleges with open arms and also made friends there.

All the competitions were carried out in a good spirit and the students dressed their best to represent their college well.

CHAPTER TEN

LIFE GOES ON

College life has millions of memories, lakhs of fights, thousands of arguments, hundreds of sad moments & real care of friends.

A college day fills maximum colures in life journey in the form of lessons. Beginnings are usually scary and endings are usually sad, but it's everything in between that makes it all worth living.

College is the place where you find out who you are.

We will now hear a few words about college from my friends words what college meant to them

From a looser to gaining confidence that I can beat anything in life heartbreaks, getting apart and friends love care, lessons from the teachers which are precious in life and silly fights, college drams, canteen bunks from loser to achiever I learned in college. (T.krishna Dinesh)

In my college days, I enjoyed myself as a kid, and I had good friends like you. Every year in life we have ups & downs I have struggled to complete assessments given lectures but it has taught me life lessons. -- (A.Mahesh)

I felt like I was different in college. I discovered what I want in life & how different should be to outstand out in life. --(Pravalika.)

We cherished very happily college & hostel life and every time we tried to make smile each other faces that's the best thing in life.--(Summit)

It was the best I can say I found my love there and got the best job there best memories best people in life.--(M.Sai Kumar)

I had a good experience, got many new friends and I got to know about how much a job and future is important. I got to know about relationship value.--(Ashiwine)

College life is one of the most memorable experiences in life. We have Assignments and case studies. Events birthdays and a lot more. We understand learning more from friends, teachers and for enemies that we can handle anything. Any moment in college is the best to reach anything and everything.--(Harsha Vardhan)

I'm lucky to have friends like them in my life.

But the sad part is,

One day this will all end.

We go in our separate ways.

We can always keep in touch but it doesn't happen.

Life gets busy with too many problems like money, job, responsibility & family.

We may not have people in our life all the time but the time we spend and memories we have will be there forever and ever.

www.ingramcontent.com/pod-product-compliance
Lightning Source LLC
Chambersburg PA
CBHW061407160726

47995CB00001B/497